Bags of
AMERICAN
FOLK
for viola

Arranged and written by
Mary Cohen

© 2010 by Faber Music Ltd
This edition first published in 2010
Bloomsbury House 74-77 Great Russell Street London WC1B 3DA
Music processed by Jeanne Roberts
Cover designed by Lydia Merrills–Ashcroft
Illustration by Andy Cooke
Printed in England by Caligraving Ltd
All rights reserved

ISBN10: 0-571-53417-1
EAN13: 978-0-571-53417-3

To buy Faber Music publications or to find out about the full range of titles available
please contact your local music retailer or Faber Music sales enquiries:

Faber Music Ltd, Burnt Mill, Elizabeth Way, Harlow CM20 2HX
Tel: +44 (0) 1279 82 89 82   Fax: +44 (0) 1279 82 89 83
sales@fabermusic.com   fabermusic.com

Foreword

Bags of American Folk is an introduction to the wonderful world of traditional music – favourite tunes passed down from one generation to the next, many from the early pioneer days. This collection has been carefully selected to include music of many different styles and moods, and it is great to play without needing any accompaniment, although you might like to form a viola band with your friends.

Folk music is always changing and developing, and there are lots of ways to personalise tunes once you have mastered the notes. For instance, you can add slides and grace notes, and your own special dynamics. Learn some of these melodies by heart and you will always have something to play for friends and family!

Contents

Down in Demerara	3	Clementine	10
Li'l Liza Jane	3	On top of Old Smokey	10
The old grey goose	3	I'se the b'y that builds the boat	10
Little red wagon	4	The Yellow Rose of Texas	11
Charlie's sweet	4	Who did?	11
The streets of Laredo	4	O Susanna	11
Four in a boat	5	Red River Valley	12
She'll be coming round the mountain	5	Steal away	12
Yankee Doodle	5	The shanty boys in the pine	12
I had a cat	6	Home on the range	13
Old woman	6	John Brown's body	13
Rocky Mountain	6	La Cucaracha †	14
Simple gifts	7	She's like the swallow	14
Dixie	7	Swing low sweet chariot †	14
Boatmen dance, boatmen sing	8	Arkensas traveller	15
Nobody knows	8	Shenandoah	15
Jubilee	8	Mexican hat dance †	15
My Grandfather's clock	9	Casey Jones	16
O when the saints	9	Puttin' on the blue check shirt ††	16
Jeannie with the light brown hair	9		

† These pieces are compatible with *Bags of American Folk for Violin* only. Everything else can be played together with *Bags of American Folk for Violin* and *Bags of American Folk for Cello*.

†† This piece is compatible with the cello book only.

Down in Demerara

Moochin' about

Li'l Liza Jane

Happily

The old grey goose

Spreading the news!

4

Little red wagon

Rolling along

Charlie's sweet

With singing tone

The streets of Laredo

Sad and thoughtful

Four in a boat

Lively

She'll be coming round the mountain

Cheerfully

Yankee Doodle

Bright and dandy!

I had a cat

Happily

Old woman

Teasing

Rocky Mountain

Pleading!

Simple gifts

Joyfully

Dixie

Enthusiastically

Boatmen dance, boatmen sing

Lively

Nobody knows

With great feeling

Jubilee

Steady and rhythmic

My Grandfather's clock

Henry Clay Work

O when the saints

Jeannie with the light brown hair

Stephen Foster

Clementine

With strong feeling

On top of Old Smokey

Lazily

I'se the b'y that builds the boat

Brightly

The Yellow Rose of Texas

With determination

Who did?

Energetically

O Susanna

Stephen Foster

Whimsically

12

Red River Valley

With singing tone

Steal away

Steadily, and with feeling

The shanty boys in the pine

Proud and bold!

Home on the range

Happily

John Brown's body

In march time

La Cucaracha

She's like the swallow

Swing low sweet chariot

Arkensas traveller

Colonel Sandford C. Faulkner

Just fast enough . . .

Shenandoah

Smoothly flowing

Mexican hat dance

Very rhythmic

Casey Jones

Steaming along!

Puttin' on the blue check shirt

Mary Cohen